Dreaming of You

words and illustrations by
gana meharii

gana meharii

dreaming of you

gana meharii

dreaming of you

chapters

---

gana meharii

dedication:

*this book is dedicated to my husband.
you supported me and made so many
small sacrifices along the way so that i
could pursue my dream of writing my
first book of poetry. you are amazing
beyonds words and selfless beyond
measure. none of this would have been
possible without you.*

chapter one

the
moon
and
stars

i stared up
at the night's sky
breathing out
my anxiety
crossing my fingers
hoping
that somehow fate
would lead you
to me

there were times
when i couldn't even
look into your eyes
for fear of blushing

my thoughts
drift towards you

i just can't seem
to keep you
off my mind

take your heart
gently in your hands
caress it
do not let the world
leave you bruised
stay strong

i have spent so much time
searching
that i don't know
if i would recognize
what i'm looking for
if i found it

dreaming of you

all of the infinity
among the galaxies
in the night's sky
could not compare
to the depth
of my love
for you

dreaming of you

all at once it felt

safe, yet dangerous
normal, yet risky
loving, yet lustful
pure, yet dirty

the first time
our lips
touched

gana meharii

does she love you
like i loved you?

no, she doesn't
because nobody ever could.

we had
our own language
our own special magic
between us
something no one else
could ever have

what we had
was ours
and ours alone

you remind me
of a warm cup of tea
on a rainy Tuesday afternoon
back in london

dreaming of you

all i ask
is that you look at me
like i'm the only thing
in the entire universe
that matters

show me you care
make me feel your love
as long as your sun
continues to shine
our love will grow
to a beautiful garden

dear god
let me be with
the one i love
for all eternity

grant me this, i pray
so that my heart
may at last rest
and cease its endless aching

everything felt different
with you
in some ways
i can't even explain

it felt like living
in a wonderful movie
the colors and sounds
created to perfection

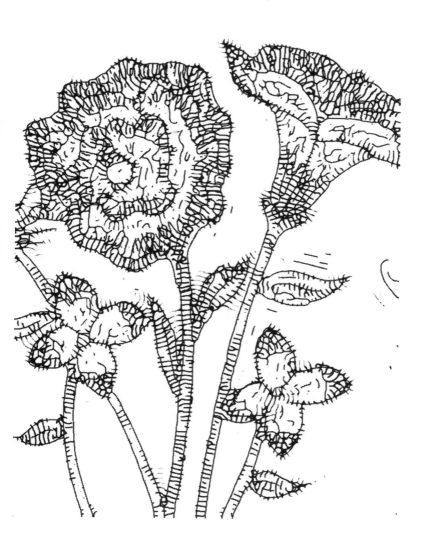

gana meharii

i find myself writing for you and only you
hoping you'll pick up this book
and find in it
pieces of yourself
for everything, it seems
goes back to you

dreaming of you

you are the only one
who sees me
the way
i wish
i could see myself

you make me believe
i could be
the version of myself
i always believed
i could be

teach me to trace my fingers
along the scars
careless lovers
left on your heart

i want to heal
every cut
and every bruise

i promise you
i will never hurt you
the way
you've been hurt
before

gana meharii

i knew
my heart
was in a perilous position
when i found myself
counting the minutes
between your texts

dreaming of you

if i could take all
of your pain
and all
of your brokenness
and bear your burdens
myself

i would do it
in a heartbeat

chapter two

aquarius

he may have broken you
but your inner light
is far stronger
than anything
he could ever do to you

the moon
is in
its fullest phase

my spirit
rises
with the tides
the aquarius
finally feels free

though it may not feel
like it right now
you have a future
and you will go
far beyond
where you are right now

nothing can truly hurt you
as long as you have
hope.

you taught me
to see life
in a whole new way
like i had never seen it
before

you opened my eyes
and i felt
like a newborn baby
seeing the world
for the first time

you make everything
so much more
beautiful

dreaming of you

lately life has felt
cloudy and confusing
like peering across the sea
through a heavy mist

clarity is elusive;

all i can do
is cling to the shore
waiting
for the sun
to rise
and clear the mist
with the new day

just hold on, just hold on.

nothing
could be more perfect
in the entire world
than the simple joy
of drinking coffee
with you
in the morning
after a long night
of making love

dreaming of you

growing pains
may hurt now
but they signal
the coming
of brighter days

so take heart
as you go
through the tunnel

take heart
for the light
will always come.

everything was dark
i felt weightless
as if i was floating
in the stars

i caught sight of a glowing door
and tried my best
to float towards it

your love
guided me through
the darkness

never forget
where you came from.

do not forget
that a flower needs roots
to keep it from
blowing away
in the wind

and you need roots
to hold you down
when things get hard

dreaming of you

gana meharii

you are my strength
when i am weak
you are my shield
when arrows fly
you are my hope
when all is dark
and you are my god
who will never let me go

remember
in your darkest moments
that the night
cannot go on
forever

remember
in your pain
that you will
one day
be healed

loving you
feels like
speeding down the highway
with the top down
singing along to the radio
at the top of our lungs

regret is a useless thing.
it does not change the past
it only causes us
to feel pain
because of it

so let go of your regret
unchain your soul
unfurl your wings
the new day has come
and it is time to be free.

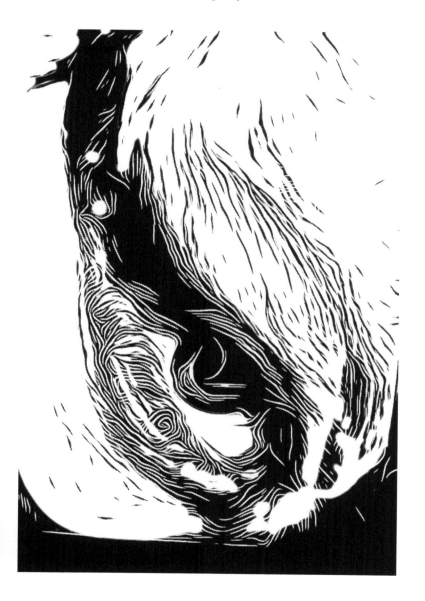

dreaming of you

love
is like a fine wine

do not hasten too quickly
to partake of it

let it breathe
and you will enjoy it
al the more

there is nothing
more beautiful
than the feeling
of laying
on your chest
comfortably
quietly

nothing feels more
like love
than this simple moment

contentment.

that's what i feel
as you run
your fingers
through my hair.

contentment.

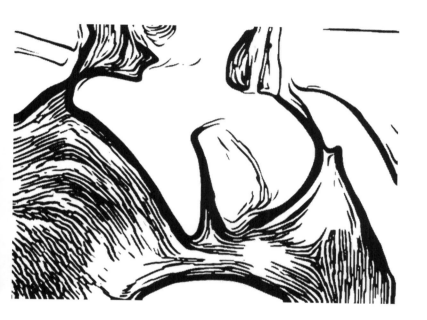

gana meharii

i love the way
you experience life

your joy
entangles with my soul
and i feel
so much happier
when i'm with you

you give
my heart
wings

the answers to all things
will eventually come
we need not distress
over the questions of life
we need only live it
and learn to be at peace.

it is important
to keep singing
even though the dark times

do not lose your joy
for it is the
most powerful thing
you have.

gana meharii

your inner joy
cannot be taken from you
by anyone else

you have to surrender it
willingly
and choose to let it die

do not do so.
hold on
to your inner joy
and let it nourish you.

be strong
even when it's not
easy

for when it's most difficult
is when it means the most
to be strong

be grateful for when life
gets hard

for it teaches you
perseverance
and gives you
the ability
to stay strong
through even
the darkest of times

gana meharii

our pain, our suffering
it will all fade away

even when life
sucks
we have to hold on
to hope

dreaming of you

chapter three

sacred
dreams

gana meharii

when i was at my lowest point
broken and destitute
you reached down to me
and gave me love

there were so many things
we never fully internalized
from our childhoods

we are merely the products
of so many past traumas

death
is not just
the end of life

death
is what happens
when you stop
believing
and hoping
that things
can become
beautiful

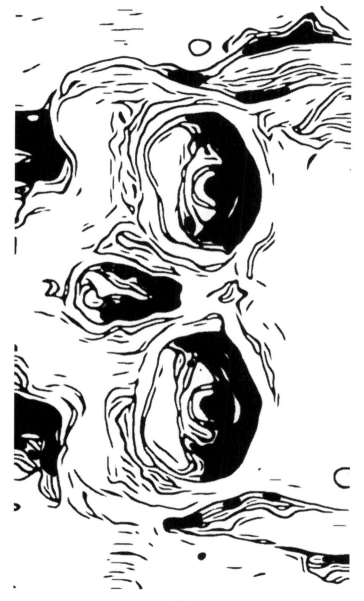

dreaming of you

gana meharii

all of the fear
all of the anxiety
all of the depression
within my brain

i wish i could dig in
to those treacherous lobes
and pick out
all of the deficiencies
that cause me
so much pain

dreaming of you

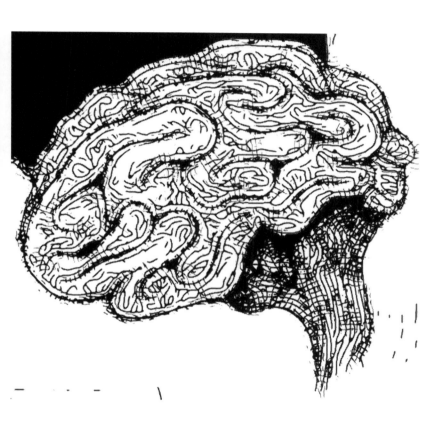

gana meharii

breathe in
breathe out
let your mind
wander

search
for a higher level
of awareness

it was never about you
all those words i said
that i wish i could take back

it was about
my own insecurities
my own flaws
afraid that you would treat me
the way the worst parts of me
think
i deserve
to be treated

but you
would never do that
to me

gana meharii

you may feel down

but remember
the only direction
that matters in life
is onward

dreaming of you

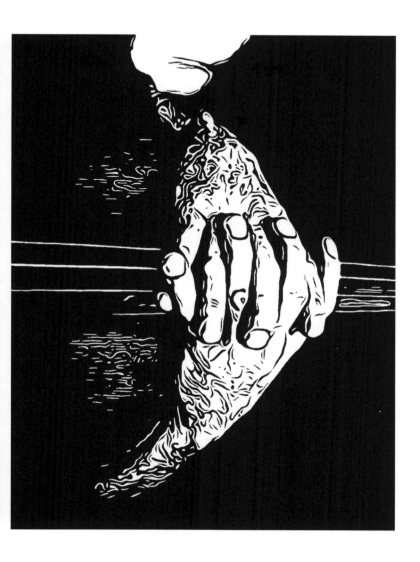

gana meharii

i imagine once more
our silhouettes against the sunset
at the edge of the ocean
the waves crashing on the shore

i imagine once more
a moment so perfect
it haunts me to this day

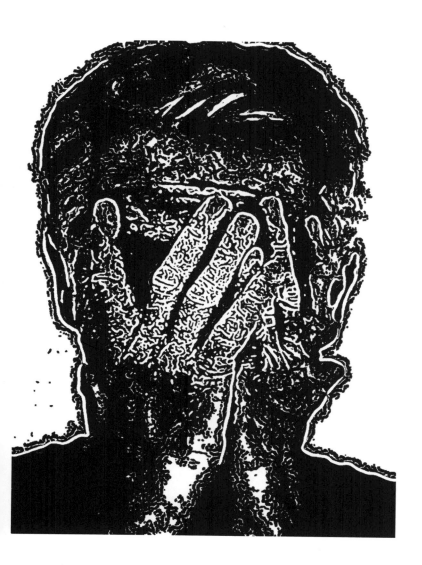

gana meharii

it is so important
sometimes
to retreat
back into yourself
away from others

search for yourself
tap into your own peace

never stop questioning
the way things are

even when
the world's evils
seem to be written
in cement

never lose hope
that we can choose
a better future

gana meharii

a plant
begins as a seed
which does not see
the light
of the sun
until
it fights
its way through
the soil

take me back
to that one night
where everything
just felt
so simple

it was just
you and i
and nothing else
mattered
in the whole world

be with someone
who lights up
your life

as you left
i whispered
"i love you"
hoping the gentle breeze
would carry it
from my heart
to yours

gana meharii

take all the photos
you can
in the moment

you never know
when that photograph
will be all you have left
of a person or place
in your life

you
are a beautiful flower
just waiting
to bloom

gana meharii

we spent the whole night
talking
and before i knew it
the sun was up again
and it was time
to say goodbye

there is no
greater peace
in my life
than the wonderful moments
i get to spend
with you

nothing feels
so perfect
as your company
plain and simple

chapter four

stars align

gana meharii

i have never felt
so lucky
in my life
as i feel
getting
to love you

gana meharii

you left me a vase of flowers
on my dresser
for me to wake up to

the bedsheets still smelled
like you
and i smiled
as i took a flower
in my hand

i love the way
you playfully protest
when i take your hoodies

i just want to keep
smelling you
so i can have
a piece of you
when you're away

you would not look
at the knife
that cut you
expecting it
to heal you

so do not look
at the people
who hurt you
expecting them
to heal you

we have only two choices
in this life

to live a life
of absolute freedom
taking everything
as it comes

or a life
of absolute enslavement
to routines and patterns

i know which one
i want.

dreaming of you

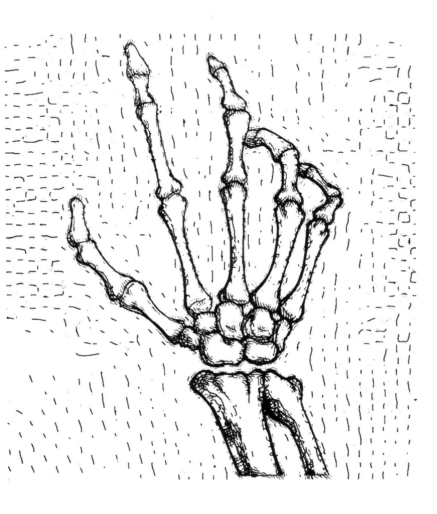

you poured gasoline
on my heart
and threw a lit match
onto it
without a care

and then have the
sheer audacity
to complain
that i burn
too brightly

dreaming of you

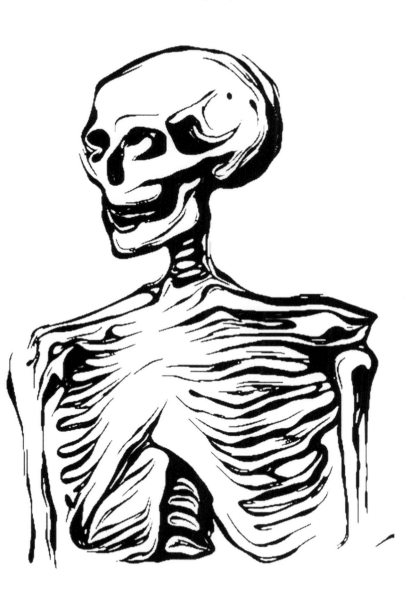

never be afraid to cry.

there is nothing like
letting out
your every emotion
to a sad song
or a sad movie

just let yourself feel
and let your heart be cleansed
by your tears
as your body
is cleansed by the rain.

dreaming of you

only with you am i truly myself. only with
you am i truly vulnerable.

dreaming of you

you make me feel comfortable in my
skin the way no one ever has before

gana meharii

we were meant
for each other

two broken souls
drifting through life
waiting for the stars to align
and bring us together

being with you
feels like
laying in a field
of flowers
all the time

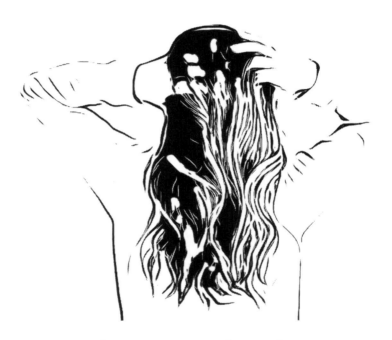

you always encouraged me to keep
drawing and writing even when
everyone else told me i was wasting my
time.

dreaming of you

i would give anything in life
to jump back into these photographs
and taste these lost moments
one last time

look to the light
breathe in
the fresh, cool air

leave your fingerprints
on the window

experience
this moment
with me

dreaming of you

trace your fingers along my spine
i want to feel your fingertips
as they give me shivers

connect the dots between my freckles
tell me the patterns you see
i want you to know every inch of me

dreaming of you

the problem with you leaving
is that you
were the only one
who ever truly
understood me

gana meharii

i dream of the day
i will walk down the aisle
towards you
with flowers in hand
and my dress flowing in the breeze

i dream of our future
and all the moments
i will cherish all the more
with you by my side

you saw me for more
than my mistakes

you saw me as a kaleidoscope
of beauty and art

you saw me as beautiful
when others didn't notice me at all

you made me see beauty in the mirror
instead of flaws and pain

dreaming of you

125

my head crowned with flowers, you
danced with me at two in the morning
under the moonlight

i want to fill my body with tattoos
i want to become a canvas
of ideas and art

i will never forget how the first rose you
gave me smelled like love and looked
like magic

you are my rosebud, the love that
waited through the long winter and
through every struggle to bring me the
most complete joy as spring bloomed

with you, my darling, the butterflies are
never in short supply

you make me feel as free as a bird
on the first winds of summer

you called me your muse
but the secret of it all
was that you
were always my muse
even when
you didn't know it

the roses you give me may physically
die
but the love they represent
will live forever within me

breathe in the universe and breathe out
peace. that is all that has ever been and
all that will ever be.

you make me feel
strong enough
to take on anything
in the entire universe

you make me feel
like a lioness

dreaming of you

the patterns of the entire universe and
the grand design of the cosmos all
conspired to create you. do not doubt for
a second that all of your strife, all of your
struggles, all of your pain is taking you
on exactly the right path to your ultimate
peace and happiness. hold on, and
never give up.

you are more
than your mistakes

you will move on
you will keep living
you will forget

do not be afraid
for even the darkness nights
have an end.

gana meharii

your lips hovered so closely to mine
the moment stretched into infinity
my senses aflame as my lips
begged to touch yours

your hands
against my skin
my body aches
for your touch

the stars and planets aligned so
perfectly to bring our souls together. i
pray that nothing will ever drive us
apart.

nothing less than the life force of the
universe itself has pushed our souls
together

death is not the end.

death is only a necessary step
in a never ending cycle

without death, there could be no life

do not grieve for the dead
take joy in the fact
that they live on
as part
of the greater whole
of the universe

dreaming of you

gana meharii

when i am with you
inspiration and passion
emanate from the vibrations
between us

everything comes alive
everything becomes art

and i, a mere spectator
touch it with my pen

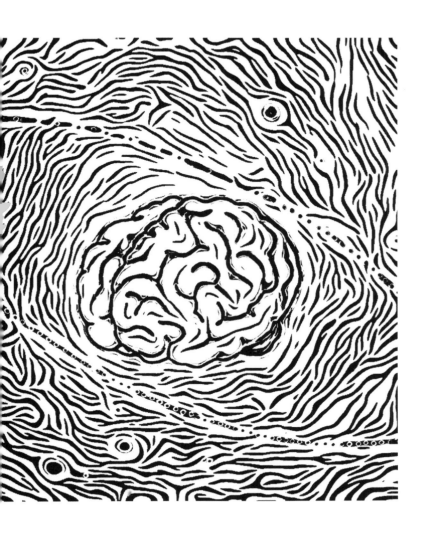

i am ashamed of how quickly and
completely i fell for you. but luckily, your
pure intentions kept me safe.

with you, the simplest things became
incredible adventures. an errands trip
into the city became endless fun. with
you, life feels so much more than
ordinary.

before we fell in love, i remember the feeling of disgust i felt when other men tried to use me for sex. i felt my desire wilt like a malnourished flower, as my spirit recoiled from those who only wanted to take from me.

but with you, as i feel your soul entangled with mine as we make love, i feel nothing but complete desire. i want to fulfill your every desire and express my love for you physically. there is nothing i wouldn't do.

when you're in love, it's that simple.

dreaming of you

gana meharii

chapter five

love
&
adoration

gana meharii

saturn and mars aligned
to make me feel
the purest joy
today

to commune with the universe
is the greatest power
we possess
as human beings

gana meharii

true love
never takes away
from your freedom

true love
is choosing
to be loyal and good
even when
you don't have to

dreaming of you

the light
does not seem
so far away
these days

i remember when it felt
as distant
as the stars
in the sky

but now
i feel
as if
i could almost
reach out
and touch it

i love to look back
at the way
people in the past
used to envision
the future

i love their optimism
their belief
that any problem
could be solved

i hope
that we can recapture
our belief
as a species
in the possibility
of utopia

for how can we reach
for utopia
if we don't believe
it's possible?

gana meharii

i love the way
you tease me
so playfully

i love the way
you sneak your hands
into my pants
when we are alone
in the back
of a movie theater

i love our scandalous passion
the fun we always have
and how good it feels
to get release
after a long day
of teasing each other

dreaming of you

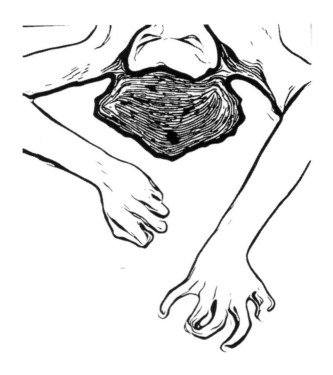

clutching at the bed sheets
i fell deeper in love with you

talk with me through the ins and outs of
the universe. let us find ourselves by
looking into infinity.

gana meharii

as you said you loved me, it felt as if i
became nothing but pure energy, pure
expression of a soul desperate for yours

164

dreaming of you

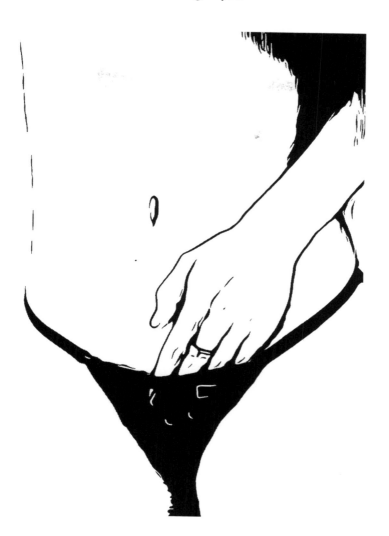

every night when i can't sleep, my
thoughts turn to you

there is no greater pleasure
than to spend
all of life's small, simple moments
with the one i love

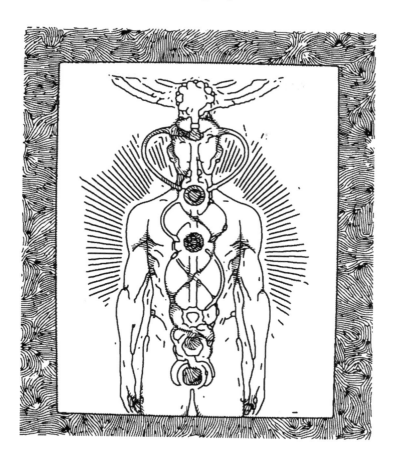

our love is so much more than something ordinary. our love could set the universe aflame with passion and bring the rotations of the galaxies to a halt. with you, my love, i feel like anything is possible.

you and i, my darling
i promise you this
i promise you forever
and every forever
after that

my all, my everything
my eternity
everything i am
is yours
now and forever.

gana meharii

you bring me hope when life feels
overwhelming

you make things make sense
when all is confusing

you make me feel brave
when fear whispers to me in the night

you make me feel
powerful

gana meharii

about this book

"dreaming of you" is gana meharii's debut book of poetry, prose, and illustrations. it is a fresh and unique take on life and love in the modern world.

love must be earned by heartbreak. peace must be earned through struggle. light cannot be earned without the anguish of darkness. and healing must be earned by overcoming pain. gana meharii's poetry and prose takes the reader on a journey through the worst aspects of life in order to fully appreciate the best when it comes.

this is a book of dreams. a book of hope, a book of love. a collection of windows into the soul of the poetess herself. 'dreaming of you' dares to ask what life can be when we reach for the stars, never taking no for an answer.

gana meharii

32011290R00103

Printed in Poland
by Amazon Fulfillment
Poland Sp. z o.o., Wrocław